Vintage Christmas Coloring

new seasons®
a division of Publications International, Ltd.

Let's get social!

 @Publications_International

 @PublicationsInternational

www.pilbooks.com

It's the best time of the Year

this is YOUR YEAR to sparkle

Enjoy Winter time

Believe iN tHe Magic Of CHRiStMaS

Joyful merry & blessed

Have yourself a Merry little Christmas

Shine Bright

making SPiRiTS bright

CHRISTMAS CHEER

HERE COMES Santa CLAUS

HEAVEN
&
NATURE
Sing

Silent Night Holy Night

'twas the night before christmas...

Meet me under the mistletoe

walking in a winter wonderland

the first noel

dashing through THE SNOW

Sparkle

ALL THE

Way

Good tidings of Comfort & Joy

I'll be home for CHRISTMAS

Santa Claus

IS COMING TO

TOWN

>>> <<<

Rocking AROUND THE Christmas TREE

MERRY CHRISTMAS TO ALL & to all a goodnight

MERRY CHRISTMAS!

let
heaven
and
nature
sing

Warm and cozy

REPEAT the sounding JOY

May your Days be Merry and Bright

Baby it's Cold outside

We wish you a Merry Christmas

BLESSINGS abound

Noël

season's
greetings

IT'S NOT WHAT'S

under the tree

THAT MATTERS

it's who's gathered

AROUND IT

Warm winter wishes

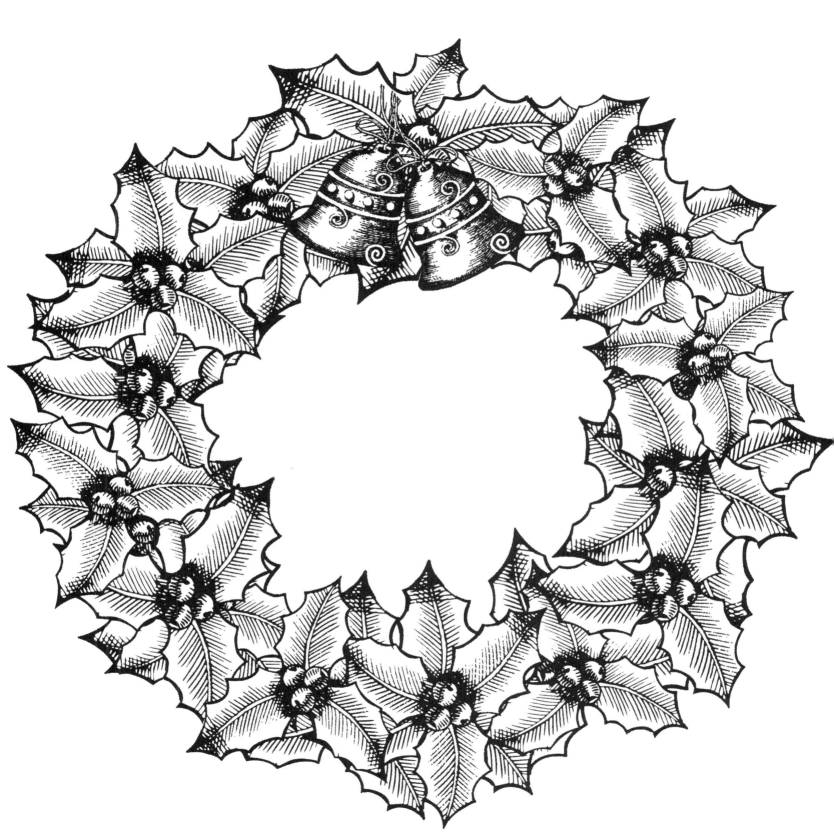